A Community Based Approach to Countering Radicalization

A Partnership for America

By Dr. Hedieh Mirahmadi
With Mehreen Farooq

WORDE
World Organization for Resource Development and Education
1875 Eye Street, NW Suite 500
Washington DC 20006
Tel: 1-202-595-1355
Fax: 1-202-318-2582
Email: staff@worde.org
Web: www.worde.org

ABOUT WORDE

World Organization for Resource Development and Education [WORDE] is a nonprofit, educational organization whose mission is to enhance communication and understanding between Muslim and non-Muslim communities and to strengthen Muslim institutions that will mitigate social and political conflict.

WORDE shapes public policy by cultivating a better understanding of Islamic ideologies that promote pluralism and service to humanity -- while exposing the roots of extremism that disrupt the peaceful coexistence of societies everywhere. WORDE specialists are academics, theologians, development experts, and policy analysts who develop effective, long-term solutions in the key areas of educational reform, resource development, and international security. Many of them serve as advisors to various US government agencies as well as international organizations and governments around the world.

ACKNOWLEDGEMENTS

We would like to thank Juan Zarate at the Center for Strategic and International Studies, Zeyno Baran at the Hudson Institute, Lorenzo Vindino at RAND Corporation, and Scott Carpenter at the Washington Institute for Near East Studies for their insightful comments. We are thankful for the ongoing cooperation with Captain Wayne Porter, Senior Advisor to Chairman of the Joint Chiefs of Staff, Deputy Chief Michael Downing, of the LA Police Department, and the valuable guidance provided throughout this project by Andy Polk, Legislative Assistant for Congresswoman Sue Myrick (R-NC-9). We would also like to express our appreciation for the support we received from Mateen Siddiqui, Vice President of the Islamic Supreme Council of America, and our many Muslim community members across the country who encouraged us to publish this report.

Front cover photo by Asim Bharwani.

CONTENTS

Executive Summary	iii
Introduction	1
History of Islamist Ideology in the US	4
Counter-Radicalization Strategies	9
Recommendations	12
Challenges	26
Conclusion	28

EXECUTIVE SUMMARY

The time has come in America for US policymakers, together with Muslim communities, to initiate a national conversation about countering the rise of homegrown radicalism and terrorism. Initiating such a partnership is an essential component of US national security given the alarming number of individuals and groups who are radicalized in America and are intent on committing violent *jihad* either in the US or abroad.

The US government's current domestic counterterrorism strategy is largely a law enforcement based approach with minimal community level involvement, predominately carried out by the FBI. We propose a shift in the approach on all sides, by increasing US government involvement at the state and local levels, as well as enlisting more public and private partners that will empower moderate Muslims[1] to be active participants. These Muslims are best positioned to counter radical narratives, however, their networks in the US—mosques, cultural associations, community centers, and college Muslim student groups—need help to develop their institutional capacity and improve their messaging capabilities.

Given that the road to radicalization within the US is largely unknown, this report is intended to be a resource for policymakers to create a new counter-radicalization strategy. The first section explores the history of radical ideology and its proliferation in the US, as a means of differentiating between deviant, misinterpreted religious tenets and the conventional beliefs of Muslims. The second section will review current strategies around the world to counter radicalization and how these programs can guide our approach at home. The third and final section will include recommendations for a way forward.

The following are some of the recommendations put forward in the report:

1. INCREASE RESEARCH IN SOCIAL SCIENCES:
Policymakers require additional research on the practice of Islam in America in order to create a diversified counter-radicalization strategy that reflects the nuances of the American Muslim population. Public and private foundations should fund research on ideologies that influence radicalization; processes of radicalization; factors for joining and leaving terrorist organizations; and deradicalization strategies led by moderate Muslims. Public opinion institutions should conduct a series of studies on the Muslim communities' attitudes towards contemporary social and political issues. Finally, public and private foundations should fund research on American Muslims' social, cultural and political demographics.

2. MOVE BEYOND GRIEVANCE BASED RELATIONS TO BUILD PARTNERSHIPS AGAINST RADICALIZATION:
Government outreach initiatives need to develop partnerships that will enable moderate Muslims to be the country's first line defense against homegrown terrorism. Community level relationships should be facilitated with thought leaders, teachers, businessmen, as well as prison and military chaplains. These relationships should be based on mutual interests beyond the scope of terrorism and community grievances, *e.g.* bullying in school, protecting children against online predators, maintaining public safety

---

[1] The term moderate Muslim is used to make a distinction between radical ideologues from the majority of Muslims who support religious freedom, non-violent conflict resolution, and the preservation of the US Constitution and rule of law. The foundational principles that differentiate these two groups are further outlined in the second section of this paper "History of Islamist Ideology in the US." It should be noted that the term "moderate" should not be conflated with social or political attitudes (*e.g.* moderate Muslims can be socially liberal or very conservative), nor should it be associated with the degree to which one practices Islam.

and engendering public service. Federal, state and local law enforcement agencies should utilize these relationships to establish a series of two-way dialogues, constructive debates, and brainstorming sessions to develop a community-based response to radicalism.

3. **DEFINE A SET OF SHARED VALUES:**
Public-private partnerships specifically created to counter-radicalization should be made with Muslims who agree on a set of shared values. Partners should support religious freedom, non-violent conflict resolution, and the preservation of the US Constitution as the rule of law. Moreover, they should reject three key principles of radical ideologues: religious intolerance, the centrality of military *jihad* to Islamic practices, and the imposition of Islamist law in the US legal system.

4. **ENCOURAGE COMMUNITY-LED, EARLIER INTERVENTIONS**
Community-led interventions should be facilitated to stop radicalization in its initial stages. Many Muslim scholars and community leaders are capable of providing legitimate counseling, counter-radicalization programming, and religious retraining in an authentic religious paradigm that is palatable to at-risk Muslims. In addition to countering radical ideology, community-led interventions should address social alienation. Public and private foundations should fund community centers that foster a sense of belonging; engage in sports and creative arts; and provide access to mentors who preach socially responsible definitions of what it means to be "good Muslim" based on shared American and Islamic values.

5. **EMPOWER MUSLIMS TO COUNTER RADICAL IDEOLOGY**
In Muslim-majority countries, moderate Muslims have a strong network of established institutions through which they conduct counter-radicalization programs. Unfortunately, in the US, such networks are not as well-institutionalized. Public and private partnerships should look to strengthen the capacity of moderate Muslim networks by investing in leadership and good governance training, institutional capacity building, as well as media and communications development. Moreover, counter-radicalization efforts of local mosque communities should be publically recognized by government officials in their speeches, dinner receptions, and award ceremonies. Highlighting the powerful voice of Muslim leaders who work diligently to discourage violence and promote pluralism, will illustrate a positive example for Muslim youth to emulate. In addition, partnership opportunities and increased funding from public or semi-public foundations can engender cooperation and trust between the government and Muslim groups.

6. **BUILD DERADICALIZATION RESOURCES**
Policymakers need a systematic way of identifying moderate Muslim networks that they can work with. A directory should be created of Muslim leaders and their community level cultural, civic, and religious institutions across the US. In addition, the government should create an educational forum where local community leaders, religious scholars, academics and analysts can brief policymakers about Islamic ideologies, the pathways to radicalization, and community-led solutions to counter radicalization.

7. **INITIATE A PUBLIC AWARENESS CAMPAIGN**
Given the increased attention of homegrown terrorism in the media, and the misunderstandings between Muslims and non-Muslims in America, it is important to engage in a public, national dialogue to counter the misperception that all Muslims are radical. Policymakers in the White House and on Capitol Hill need to draw media attention to the effort and organize public forums where the threat of domestic radicalization can be addressed along with the differences between radical and mainstream religious tenets of Islam. Similarly, public and private foundations should provide resources for Muslims to

convene and discuss organic, bottom-up, counter-radicalization efforts within their communities. Throughout this process, Muslim groups should develop public awareness campaigns against radicalization – issuing statements against radical ideologies that breed violence and hatred; and publishing pamphlets and booklets that highlight Islamic values of religious tolerance, pluralism, gender equality, and social cohesion.

8. CONFRONT RADICALIZATION ONLINE

The internet is an increasingly significant vehicle for radicalizing Muslims in America. In addition to the efforts that are already being undertaken to reduce the number of radical websites, there is an opportunity for local Muslim leaders, imams and scholars to produce moderate, counter-radical websites to educate Muslims on mainstream Islam and to discredit extremist arguments. At the same time, local community centers and mosques should hold special radical propaganda awareness programs to discuss the dangers of online indoctrination with young Muslims.

CONCLUSION

While there are a number of routes to radicalization, an undeniable driving force is the propagation of radical ideologies. Policymakers will have to look beyond the traditional law enforcement approaches in which authorities intervene just before or after an act of terror. Instead, domestic resources should be expanded to support community-led initiatives by moderate Muslims that deter individuals from radicalizing in the first place. Investing in research will also help us understand the threat of radicalization better. This approach will save lives and taxpayer dollars. Law enforcement agencies will also have to move beyond grievance-based forums of engagement to creating partnerships with Muslims who will lead the struggle against domestic radicalization. These partnerships will move us towards a safer future.

INTRODUCTION

The recent controversy over building an Islamic center within two blocks of Ground Zero has catapulted the American Muslim community to an unprecedented level of public scrutiny -- even more so than after 9-11.[2] This phenomenon is partly the result of the US Government and the Muslim communities' failure to address the rise of radicalism head-on. On one hand, both the Obama and Bush administrations have left "Islam" out of the equation when discussing terrorism committed by Muslims in an effort to show respect towards the majority of American Muslims who abhor violence committed in the name of Islam.[3] On the other hand, Muslim communities have been hesitant to acknowledge the threat of radicalization amongst their members. Avoiding the issue has increased misconceptions of Islam and obfuscated the American public's ability to distinguish the radicals from mainstream, moderate Muslims.[4] The time has come in America for US policymakers, together with Muslim communities, to initiate a national conversation about countering the rise of homegrown radicalism and terrorism. We realize that many Muslim activists or leaders may be reticent to identify the problem as related to a particular sect, with some Islamic foundation, but the Muslim community needs to take ownership of this problem and become part of the solution.

Initiating a national conversation on countering radicalization is an essential component of US national security given the alarming number of individuals and groups who are radicalized in America[5] and are intent on committing violent *jihad* either in the US or abroad.[6]

Examples of recent domestic radicalization highlighted in the media:

- Derrick Shareef was inspired by radical Islamist ideologues to attempt to carry out an attack on the Cherry Vale Mall in Rockford, Illinois in December 2006.[7]
- In January 2007, **Shahawar Matin Siraj**, who regularly visited an Islamist bookstore known as an "extremist incubator," was given a sentence of 30 years for conspiracy to bomb a 34th street subway station in New York City.[8]
- In May 2007, a group of six men – allegedly avid viewers of violent, *jihadi* videos - obtained weapons and planned an attack on Fort Dix military base in New Jersey.[9]

---

[2] "In US, Religious Prejudice Stronger Against Muslims," *GALLUP,* January 21, 2010, http://www.gallup.com/poll/125312/religious-prejudice-stronger-against-muslims.aspx

[3] For the purpose of clarity, we specifically cite to terrorism committed by "Muslims" as distinct from other terror groups such as white supremists or eco-terrorists, not because the latter does not exist but because this paper is specifically addressing the issue of terrorism arising from Muslims.

[4] The term moderate Muslim is used to make a distinction between radical ideologues and the majority of Muslims who support religious freedom, non-violent conflict resolution, and the preservation of the US Constitution as the rule of law. The foundational principles that differentiate these two groups are further outlined in the second section of this paper "History of Islamist Ideology in the US." It should be noted that the term "moderate" should not be conflated with social or political attitudes (*e.g.* moderate Muslims can be socially liberal or very conservative), nor should it be associated with the degree to which one practices Islam.

[5] "The Domestic Terror Threat," *Newsweek,* November 19, 2009, http://www.newsweek.com/2009/11/19/the-domestic-terror-threat.html

[6] Mitchell D. Silber, Director Intelligence Analysis for the New York City Police Department, Committee Testimony for the Senate Homeland Security and Governmental Affairs Committee. November 19, 2009.

[7] "The Domestic Terror Threat," *Newsweek,* November 19, 2009, http://www.newsweek.com/2009/11/19/the-domestic-terror-threat.html

[8] Mitchel Silber and Arvin Bhatt, "Radicalization in the West," *New York City Police Department,* page 70.

- In April 2009 four men, three of whom were radicalized in US prisons attempted to bomb a Jewish Synagogue in Riverdale, NY.[10]
- In July 2009, seven men inspired by al-Qaeda armed themselves with 27,000 rounds of ammunition with the intent to attack the Marine Base in Qauntico, VA.[11]
- In September 2009, Najibullah Zazi was arrested as part of an al-Qaeda linked conspiracy to attack locations in New York City with explosives.[12]
- Later that month two separate individuals – not linked to any specific terrorist group, operating as "lone wolves" – plotted attacks on office buildings in Dallas, TX and Federal buildings in Springfield, IL.[13] According to intelligence analysts, much of their radicalization was US-based.[14]
- On May 1, 2010 Faisal Shahzad was arrested after his foiled Times Square bombing attempt. Shahzad is believed to have forged relationships with radical groups through a classmate from the University of Bridgeport, Connecticut. [15]
- One month later, on June 5, 2010, the FBI arrested Alessa and Almonte just before they boarded their planes to join the Somali terrorist organization, Al-Shabab. They were arrested for conspiring to commit acts of murder and kidnapping.[16]
- The latest, Farooque Ahmed, was arrested October 27, 2010 for plotting a terrorist attack on Washington DC-area subway stations. Ahmed told informants he wanted to complete the five pillars of Islam by attending the Hajj (Muslim pilgrimage to Mecca) before making the "top mark" as a martyr.[17]

According to a Congressional Report, "The apparent spike in such activity after May 2009 suggests that at least some Americans—even if a tiny minority—continue to be susceptible to ideologies supporting a violent form of jihad."[18] For these individuals, theological arguments based on radical interpretations of a faith legitimize, justify and encourage acts of terrorism. Although mainstream Muslims worldwide wholly condemn these radical ideologies, a small sect of extremists has been working for almost a century to use religion as a weapon of war. This enemy is not an individual or group, but rather a

---

[9] "The Domestic Terror Threat," *Newsweek,* November 19, 2009, http://www.newsweek.com/2009/11/19/the-domestic-terror-threat.html

[10] Mitchell D. Silber, Director Intelligence Analysis for the New York City Police Department, Committee Testimony for the Senate Homeland Security and Governmental Affairs Committee, November 19, 2009.

[11] "US Terror Suspects Accused of Targeting Marine Base," *Reuters*, September 24, 2009, http://www.reuters.com/article/idUSTRE58N6YT20090924

[12] Mitchell D. Silber, Director Intelligence Analysis for the New York City Police Department, Committee Testimony for the Senate Homeland Security and Governmental Affairs Committee. November 19, 2009.

[13] "Illinois Man Charged in Plot to Bomb Federal Offices," *Reuters,* September 24, 2009, http://www.reuters.com/article/idUSN2447383520090924

[14] Mitchell D. Silber, Director Intelligence Analysis for the New York City Police Department, Committee Testimony for the Senate Homeland Security and Governmental Affairs Committee. November 19, 2009.

[15] Andrea Elliot, "Militant's Path from Pakistan to Times Square," *The New York Times,* June 22, 2010, http://www.nytimes.com/2010/06/23/world/23terror.html

[16] Robert Worth, "Cleric in Yemen Admits Meeting Airliner Plot Suspect, Journalist Says," *New York Times*, January 31, 2010, http://www.nytimes.com/2010/02/01/world/middleeast/01yemen.html?ref=umar_farouk_abdulmutallab

[17] Spencer Hsu,"Suspect in DC Metro Bomb Sought to Fight US Troops Overseas, Records Say," *The Washington Post*, October 28, 2010, http://www.washingtonpost.com/wp-dyn/content/article/2010/10/28/AR2010102803082.html?sid=ST2010102705265

[18] Jerome Bjelopera and Mark A. Randol, "American Jihadist Terrorism: Combating a Complex Threat," *Congressional Research Service,* September 20, 2010.

complex transnational network of organizations that share a common ideology. This ideology radicalizes individuals, regardless of their race, ethnicity, socio-economic status, or education, and converts them into militants.

Given that the road to radicalization within the US is largely unknown, this report is intended to be a resource for policymakers to create a new counter-radicalization strategy. The first section explores the history of Islamist ideology and its proliferation in the US as a means of differentiating between deviant, misinterpreted religious tenets and the conventional beliefs of Muslims. The second section will review current strategies around the world to counter radicalization and how these programs can guide our approach at home. The third and final section will include recommendations for a way forward.

It is our belief that both public and private actors have unique opportunities to empower Muslim scholars, educators and community leaders who have clearly and consistently promoted peace, pluralism and social cohesion. These Muslims voices are best positioned to counter radical narratives within an authentic Islamic framework, and can exert pressure from within Muslim communities to moderate radical individuals and institutions. However, their networks throughout the US—including mosques, cultural associations, community centers, and college Muslim student groups—need help to develop their institutional capacity and competitive marketing skills.

Several recommendations are directed specifically to public policymakers. For example, the government can forge stronger relationships with moderate Muslim networks by broadening outreach efforts and conducting more community level dialogues. Such efforts will enable the government to identify Muslim leaders who can provide accurate cultural competency training and who can brief local and national policymakers about Islamic ideologies and the pathways to radicalization in America. In addition, the government should raise the public profile of Muslim organizations that work at the grass-roots level to decrease radicalization in their communities.

> Public and private actors have unique opportunities to empower Muslim scholars, educators and community leaders who have clearly and consistently promoted peace, pluralism and social cohesion.

Other recommendations are directed to the Muslim community at-large. In order to be treated as an honest and credible partner in countering the rise of homegrown terrorism, Muslim leaders need to be willing to address the deviant religious tenets that feed the terrorists' narrative. This should be done through a wide variety of mediums including public channels, websites, and online chat forums. If religious factors in radicalization are the purview of the community, American Muslims must demonstrate their commitment to solving it. In some cases, that requires profound humility and courage to undo the damage that was done from years of promulgating anti-social messages and/or a paranoid sense of victimization.

HISTORY OF ISLAMIST IDEOLOGY IN THE US

In order to differentiate between mainstream moderate Muslims and radical Islamists, it is important to explore the history of Islamist ideology and the main tenants that separate it from mainstream Islamic belief.

FOUNDATIONAL PRINCIPLES

Modern Islamist radicalism traces its roots back to an ideology propounded by Muhammad ibn Abd al-Wahhab (1703-1792), a self-declared scholar from central Arabia who set out with a puritanical zeal to cleanse Islamic culture and create a pure society based on his radical reinterpretation of Islam. The extreme interpretations of Islam within his doctrine, commonly referred to today as Wahhabism, have been a defining influence on the Taliban, Al-Qaeda and other radical organizations. Though *Wahhabism* has been adapted in the various countries in which it has flourished, many of the foundational principles remain the same.

Ibn Abd al-Wahhab reinterpreted Islam by disregarding the rich tradition of Islamic scholarship that shaped the four classical schools of Sunni jurisprudence, which had promoted justice and moderation in Muslim societies for centuries.[19] Instead, he advocated a revolutionary approach whereby individuals, regardless of religious education or training, would reinterpret holy texts. By decontextualizing Islamic principles and disregarding previous theological discourse, ibn Abd al-Wahhab reinterpreted Islamic scripture in a dogmatic and literalist manner. This method allowed him to justify religious intolerance, advocate extreme forms of capital punishment, and apply draconian interpretations of Islamic law. It also enabled him to label his challengers as apostates, and to use violence to promote his worldview.[20]

There are three major principles that shape the intolerant and aggressive nature of Wahhabism. First is the concept of stripping Islam of its cultural practices and traditions that are purportedly *bida'a,* a heretical innovation of Islam. Core traditional Muslim practices such as honoring saints, the performance of sacred music, and celebrating the birthday of the Prophet Muhammad were outlawed. In keeping with this belief, Wahhabi clerics have

> **Radical Islamist Principles**
>
> There are three major principles that shape the intolerant and aggressive nature of Wahhabism.
>
> First is the concept of stripping Islam of its cultural practices and traditions that are purportedly *bida'a,* a heretical innovation of Islam.
>
> Second is the concept of *takfirism,* the radical belief that any Muslim who does not practice Islam – as they define it – is deemed an unbeliever and may be killed.
>
> Third is the understanding of what defines *jihad.* Militant Wahhabis selectively cite verses of the Quran to justify waging a "holy war" to promote their brand of Islam.

---

[19] William Cleveland, *A History of the Modern Middle East, 2004,* Colorado: Westview Press, page 123.
[20] Madawi, page 4.

destroyed the burial places of the Prophet Muhammad's family, despite their sacred significance to Muslims worldwide. Elsewhere, they have destroyed saints' shrines and prohibit the visitation of graves, claiming that it promotes idol worship. Today, militant groups influenced by Wahhabi ideology have targeted and killed thousands of Muslims for engaging in *bida'a*.

Second is the concept of *takfirism,* the radical belief that any Muslim who does not practice Islam – as theydefine it – is deemed an unbeliever and may be killed. This doctrine has been used by many militant groups across the globe to kill innocent Muslims who do not accept their agenda. It is a doctrine that stands in direct contrast to the classical Islamic belief that tolerance, diversity and pluralism strengthen society.[21] For Wahhabis, the label of "non-believer" also extends to Jews and Christians who are traditionally respected in Islam as "believers," or "People of the Book" for having received similar messages by God. These two principles of demonizing the "other"—whether its fellow Muslims or people of other faiths—is what makes this ideology so dangerous. It is a culture of hatred that often leads to violence and stands in staunch opposition to the universal right of religious freedom and tolerance.

Third is the understanding of what defines *jihad.* Historically, *jihad* has meant "to struggle in the way of God." According to traditions of the Prophet Muhammad and his companions, *jihad* traditionally means both an internal struggle to control one's ego to submit to the will of God, as well as a single instance of combative *jihad*, which can only be implemented in accordance with strict principles of warfare. Nonetheless, militant Wahhabis ignore the principles and rules required to wage external *jihad* and instead selectively cite verses of the Quran to justify waging a "holy war" to promote their brand of Islam. Their targets include non-believers, non-practicing Muslims, and people whom they believe are enemies of the *ummah,* the worldwide Muslim community. Militant Wahhabis have even waged *jihad* on Saudi Arabia. In 1979 militants instigated a violent takeover of the holy city of Mecca during the annual pilgrimage because they believed that the Saudi government's modernization initiatives – in particular the use of Western teachers in religious schools, women in the media, and the spread of television – were unIslamic.[22] Although the government was able to halt the siege within two weeks, the state acquiesced to curtail modernization, and appropriated greater funding towards cleric-missionaries throughout the Islamic world.

---

[21] According to classical interpretations of the importance of tolerance and pluralism, the Qur'an teaches "among Allah's signs are the variations in your languages and your colors," Chapter 30:22.
[22] Yaroslav Trofimov, *The Siege of Mecca: The Forgotten Uprising in Islam's Holiest Shrine and the Birthplace of Al-Qaeda*, Double Day, 2007.

THE SPREAD OF WAHHABI IDEOLOGY

In 1744, Muhammad ibn Abd al-Wahhab forged an alliance with the politically ambitious Muhammad ibn Saud. The Al Saud tribal family afforded ibn Abd al-Wahhab protection and endorsed his dogmatic interpretation of Islam. In return, the Al Saud received political legitimacy and support from ibn Abd al-Wahhab's disciples. Together, they were able to gain influence by waging successful military campaigns and by offering Arabian tribes material assistance in the form of agricultural supplies. Communities that vowed their allegiance to the Saudi family were provided mosques and scholars to disseminate the Wahhabi doctrine.[23] Even after the deaths of Muhammad ibn Abd al-Wahhab and Muhammad ibn Saud, the religious-political alliance has continued.[24]

With the oil discoveries in the 1930s, the Saud family and Wahhabi ideology grew in global significance. It was not until the 1979 Soviet invasion of Afghanistan, however, that violent Wahhabism become a global phenomenon. During the war, Wahhabi-centric groups increased their recruitment efforts for the "holy war" in Afghanistan by opening enlistment offices and training camps throughout the world, indoctrinating thousands with radical ideologies. After the war ended, the cadre of Wahhabist militants fighting in Afghanistan sought new battlegrounds in Bosnia, Somalia, Chechnya, Pakistan, and Yemen.

Wahhabi thought has proliferated outside of Saudi Arabia and has influenced numerous political groups both with violent and professed non-violent platforms, including the Muslim Brotherhood in Egypt and their off-shoots across the Middle East, the Jamaat Islami in Pakistan and the Tablighi Jama`at, a group that claims purely missionary objectives, but whose promulgated belief system has led many of its followers to eventually move on to terrorist groups. These movements commonly call for a restoration of "God's sovereignty" through the establishment of a *Caliphate*, or a Muslim state devoid of secular laws. Advocating the use of armed *jihad*,[25] their goal is to "re-Islamize" Muslim communities through violent revolution and the imposition of Wahhabi-inspired *Sharia* law.[26] Many moderate Muslims fear that once these groups are empowered they will subvert the democratic process, reduce women's rights and discriminate against non-Muslims.[27]

Since many of these groups do not self-identify themselves with Wahhabism, analysts often opt to use the term *Islamism* instead to denote the difference between this political ideology rooted in deviant interpretations of Islamic doctrine and mainstream Islamic beliefs. Practically speaking, Islamism is not significantly doctrinally different than Wahhabism and both are global expansionist doctrines. However, the term *Islamist* may be more applicable to describe groups whose focus is on the politics of the Muslim community rather than its religious conservatism.

> Wahhabi thought has influenced numerous political groups both with violent and professed non-violent platforms, including the Muslim Brotherhood, the Jamaat Islami and the Tablighi Jama`at,

---

[23] Cleveland, page 231.
[24] "A Chronology: The House of Saud," *Frontline,* http://www.pbs.org/wgbh/pages/frontline/shows/saud/cron/
[25] As discussed above, extremists often cite external *jihad* as a justification for waging a "holy war" against non-believers and Muslims whom they believe have deviated from the "Salafi" or pure practices of the faith.
[26] Sharifa Zahur, page 272
[27] Nathan Brown and Amr Hamzawy, "Draft Party Platform of the Egyptian Muslim Brotherhood," *Carnegie Papers,* January 2008. http://carnegieendowment.org/files/cp89_muslim_brothers_final.pdf

ISLAMISM IN THE US

From the 1980's through the 1990's Islamist ideology permeated American mosques, community centers, and curricula in Islamic schools[28] with the help of oil revenues from the Gulf States.[29] The strategy for proselytizing in the US was based on three mechanisms intended to foster rapid ideological change across communities.

First, numerous foundations were established by foreign financiers to provide students and preachers with scholarships and stipends to live, study, and proselytize in the US. The teachings and material disseminated by these students and preachers has been widely criticized for encouraging *jihad* and promoting religious intolerance towards non-Muslims, and even Shi'a and Sufi Muslims.[30] Some preachers were able to launch successful, aggressive campaigns to take over the leadership of mosques. Intimidation tactics were used to silence the mainstream Muslim congregations, and imams who were not conservative enough were removed from their position of authority.[31]

Second, considerable resources were spent building large mosques throughout the US in California, Missouri, Michigan, Illinois, New Jersey, New York, Ohio, Virginia and Maryland.[32] These mosques served as effective facilities where books and copies of the Quran with Islamist interpretations could be disseminated and where Islamist preachers could deliver weekly sermons to large congregations. Outside of the scope of *dawa*, the missionary call to Islam, these centers did not typically encourage social integration into broader American society *unless* it served the political purpose of gaining influence.

Third, to facilitate public engagement with policymakers, Islamists created think tanks, Islamic charities and national

> **An Islamist Three-Pronged Strategy**
>
> 1) Numerous foundations were established to provide students and preachers with scholarships and stipends to live, study, and proselytize in the US.
>
> 2) Mosques were built so that books and copies of the Quran with Islamist interpretations could be disseminated and Islamist preachers could deliver their sermons.
>
> 3) Think tanks, charities and national organizations to represent Muslim interests in the US were created to facilitate public engagement with policymakers.

---

[28] Christopher Blanchard, "The Islamic Traditions of Wahhabism and Salafiyya," *Congressional Research Services*, January 24, 2008.
[29] David Ottaway, "US Eyes Money Trails of Saudi-Backed Charities," *The Washington Post,* Thursday, August 19, 2004, Page A01.
[30] Valerie Strauss, "Critics of Saudi Academy Say Textbooks Promote Intolerance," *The Washington Post,* January 10, 2008, http://www.washingtonpost.com/wp-dyn/content/article/2008/01/09/AR2008010903338.html
[31] Akbar Ahmad, *Journey into America, the Challenge of Islam*, Washington DC: Brookings Institution Press, 2010, page 5,254.
[32] David Ottaway, "US Eyes Money Trails of Saudi-Backed Charities," *The Washington Post,* Thursday, August 19, 2004, Page A01.

organizations to represent Muslim interests in the US.[33] The strategy has been widely successful as this expansive Islamist network projects itself as the de facto voice of Islam in America.

Since September 11, 2001, several Islamist leaning foundations, mosques, research organizations and national institutions have been scrutinized for their association with extremists and terrorists –despite their efforts to moderate their rhetoric.[34] While some of these organizations might not directly participate in, or support violent extremism, the foundational principles of their ideology is exactly the same as the violent groups – they mainly differ on the means by which to accomplish those goals. For example, non-violent Islamists believe the imposition of Islamist law in Western countries will result from the democratic process and subversion of Western free societies. Violent Islamists do not typically engage in this type of "long-term civilizational *jihad*;"[35] they prefer instead to bring about the same goals through violent insurrection.[36] It is important to note that both groups may also support violence overseas in conflict areas such as Palestine, Iraq, or Afghanistan. It is for this reason the non-violent Islamist leaders and organizations can be a "slippery-slope" to greater radicalization or violent militarism.[37]

To ensure that the new counter-radicalization strategy is a partnership with the Muslim leaders and networks that share our vision for the future of America, it is important to work with Muslim groups that *reject* three key principles of radical Islamism: religious intolerance, the centrality of military *jihad* to Islamic practices, as well as the wholesale replacement of the US constitution with extreme interpretations of Islamist law. Those leaders and institutions who have truly changed their anti-American stance and have encouraged pluralism and respect for democratic values, should be brought into counter-radicalization partnerships.

---

[33] *Ibid*.
[34] Jerry Markon, "Witness is Silent in Terror Probe," *The Washington Post*, November 14, 2006, http://www.washingtonpost.com/wp-dyn/content/article/2006/11/13/AR2006111301205.html
[35] Douglas Farah, Ron Sandee and Josh Lefkowitz, "The Muslim Brotherhood in the United States: A Brief History," *NEFA Foundation*, October 26, 2007, http://counterterrorismblog.org/upload/2007/12/nefaikhwan1007%5B1%5D.pdf
[36] United States of America v. Holy Land Foundation for Relief and Development et al, No. 3:04-CR-240-G, United States District Court for the Northern Division of Texas, Dallas Division, Gov't exhibit: Government Exhibit 003-0085; 3:04-CR-240-G; U.S. v. HLF, et al. p.21.
[37] Philip Sherwell and Alex Spillius, "Fort Hood Shooting: Texas Army Killer Linked to September 11 Terrorists," *Telegraph.co.uk*, November 7, 2009, http://www.telegraph.co.uk/news/worldnews/northamerica/usa/6521758/Fort-Hood-shooting-Texas-army-killer-linked-to-September-11-terrorists.html

CURRENT COUNTER-RADICALIZATION STRATEGIES

Several countries have pursued counter-radicalization strategies from different angles, some of which focus on strengthening moderate Muslim networks as a bulwark against radical groups, and others that rely more heavily on law enforcement agencies.

In the past twenty years, the French government has invested in an approach which relies heavily on law enforcement agency interventions. For example, when the Islamist terrorist threat reached its height during the Algerian civil war, France used its intelligence agencies to disrupt terrorist networks. Today, the state continues to maintain a strong sense of police and intelligence presence through the Central Directorate of Interior Intelligence which monitors individuals with suspected ties to radical groups. A great deal of the intelligence work is carried out by undercover agents who have the capacity to "incite" one or several suspects to break the law. Suspects with even the smallest or remote connection to a terrorist plot can be apprehended and imprisoned.[38]

The Dutch government's approach moves beyond a strictly law enforcement approach to one that involves broader community engagement, particularly with local imams. The Netherlands created "information houses" that local community members can turn to, to report and seek guidance on specific at-risk individuals. The information house acts as a liaison between the law enforcement agencies and the community. They attempt to address most conflicts at the local level before the law enforcement officials are involved.[39]

The Saudi government pursues a community and family-level approach which focuses on radicalized individuals who have not yet taken violent actions. Once an individual is apprehended, imams and religious clerics are involved in providing religious re-education.[40] The Saudis offer various incentives to former detainees and their families to try to keep them from reverting to radicalism, including assistance in finding a job, helping a spouse and/or providing financial or housing assistance. Once an

---

> **Deradicalization Approaches**
>
> The French government approach relies heavily on law enforcement agency interventions.
>
> The Dutch government's approach moves beyond a strictly law enforcement approach to one that involves greater community engagement with local imams.
>
> The Saudi government pursues a community and family-level approach.
>
> The UK's bottom-up approach brings together local moderate Muslim networks and law enforcement authorities to work at the regional and district level to counter-radicalization.

---

[38] Charles Rault, "The French Approach to Counterterrorism," *CTC Sentinel,* January 2010.
[39] "Rewriting the Narrative, an Integrated Strategy for Counter-radicalization," *The Washington Institute for Near East Policy*, March 2009.
[40] Michael Jacobson, "Terrorist Dropouts, Learning from Those who have Left," *Washington Institute for Near East Policy*, Policy Focus #101, January 2010, page 17.

individual has gone through the government's program, they are required to promise never to return to a life of crime and violence, and their families are held responsible to ensure that the individual does not relapse.[41] Although the program forces the individual to renounce violence, it does not necessarily change the underlying cause for what motivated the violence in the first place: the radical ideology. As such, the Saudi program is mostly one of disengagement and not deradicalization.

Similar to Saudi Arabia's program, Singapore, Malaysia, Indonesia and Yemen have pursued a religious re-habilitation program to "de-program" radicalized individuals. The shortcoming of these approaches is that the interventions occur *after* radicalization. This approach does not consider that earlier interventions could prevent radicalization in the first place by countering radical narratives and strengthening moderate voices.

The UK's national counter-radicalization strategy, PREVENT, involves a bottom-up approach that brings together local moderate Muslim networks and law enforcement authorities to work at the regional and district level to counter-radicalization.[42] The PREVENT plan involves raising an awareness of Islamic radicalization within Muslim and non-Muslim communities (particularly focusing on at-risk youth), establishing a broad network of Muslims from across the country from different ethnic backgrounds, and establishing and strengthening existing organizations that can counter radical Islamist narratives. In addition, the program funds local organizations that can provide youth with civic education, and channel youth energy towards positive activities such as volunteering, sports and the arts.

To date, the British government has funded a number of projects such as the "Ambassadors for Islam" project which provide young Muslims with "theological arguments to counter extremist ideologies, to dispel misapprehensions and develop their role as citizens, leaders and positive role models, so that they can become 'ambassadors' for mainstream Islam and assert their British identity."[43] De-radicalization resources were created by local partners based on the Quran and prophetic traditions that focused on encouraging respect, tolerance, harmony and a positive role in the community. In order to teach civic engagement, the government invested in the development of citizenship teaching materials for Islamic schools across the country. Moreover, they strengthened the moderate Muslim voice with leadership and communications training through "Continuous Professional Development Programs" for faith leaders and workers.[44] Online, the government worked with industry partners to "scope ways of reducing access to terrorist and violent extremist-related material on the internet…[while] developing programs of work to support mainstream websites and increase the volume and profile of popular Islamic websites."[45]

The UK PREVENT program is a good model because it works with a broad spectrum of Muslim voices, opens the marketplace of ideas, and empowers local organizations. Unfortunately this has also been the program's greatest weakness. Since a wide range of organizations were encouraged to seek partnerships with the government, few benchmarks for partnerships based on shared values were imposed. The government did not adequately differentiate between moderate, mainstream Muslims and hardline

---

[41] Christopher Boucek, "Saudi Arabia's 'Soft' Counterterrorism Strategy: Prevention, Rehabilitation, and Aftercare," *Carnegie Endowment for International Peace,* September 2008, Pages 7, 17, 19.
[42] "The Prevent Strategy: A Guide for Local Partners in England; Stopping People Becoming or Supporting Terrorists and Violent Extremists," *HM Government,* June 20, 2008.
[43] *Ibid*, page 20.
[44] *Ibid*, page 19.
[45] *Ibid*, page 24.

Islamist groups. As a result, some groups that worked against state interests, desired an Islamist state in the UK, and supported violent *jihad* were empowered.[46] It was not until four years after PREVENT was initiated, that the government published updated guidelines that stipulated "Organizations funded under PREVENT need to demonstrate a commitment to our shared values."[47] Unfortunately, even this new policy has not stopped the UK government from working with unsavory groups.[48]

The lesson to be gained from the UK experience is that community level work with Muslim groups will require a better understanding of the difference between the Islam practiced by millions of moderate, mainstream Muslims and those who ascribe to radical ideologies. The US government should choose its partners carefully.

---

[46] Maajid Nawaz and Ed Husain, "Preventing Terrorism: Where Next for Britain?" *Quilliam Strategic Briefing Paper*, June 14, 2010, page 3.
[47] "Delivering the Prevent Strategy: An Updated Guide for Local Partners." *HM Government*, August 2009.
[48] Shiraz Maher and Martyn Frampton, "Choosing Our Friends Wisely: Criteria for Engagement with Muslim Groups," *Policy Exchange,* 2009.

RECOMMENDATIONS

The US government's current domestic counterterrorism approach is largely a law enforcement based approach with some community level involvement. In 2004 the National Counterterrorism Center (NCTC) was established to collect and analyze intelligence relating to counterterrorism between the FBI, Department of Homeland Security and other federal agencies.[49,50] Similar to the French government's strategy, many of the recent US homegrown terrorism suspects are apprehended by undercover agents who have spent years building up cases against the suspects. In most instances law enforcement agencies intervene and apprehend radicalized terrorist suspects just as they are about to carry out their attack, or immediately after the attack. By this point, the individual has already become radicalized.[51]

> As the number of these domestic threats is increasing, it is clear that an updated counter-radicalization strategy should be developed immediately.

In this report, we propose a shift in the approach on all sides, by increasing US government involvement at the state and local levels, as well as enlisting more public and private partnerships that will empower moderate Muslims to be active partners in countering radicalization. The following is a list of recommendations pertaining to various actors involved in a community based approach to the problem.

1. Increase Research in the Social Sciences

Some critics contend that due to the limited research available of Islamic ideologies in America, federal agencies have pursued a "bull-in-a-china-shop approach" to addressing homegrown terrorism, asking the wrong people the wrong questions in the wrong mosques.[52] The limited research is due to a number of factors. According to the Pew Research Center, quantitative data is limited because the Census cannot ask people to identify their religious or cultural heritage.[53] As a result, there has yet to even be a definitive estimate of how many Muslims live in America.[54] Furthermore, national projects that have measured public opinion and Muslim attitudes such as the Pew Research Center Poll, "Muslim Americans: Middle Class and Mostly Mainstream," and Gallup's "Muslim Americans: A National Portrait" are excellent studies, but they provided data from one point in time and don't cover an exhaustive list of topics relevant to the radicalization process. Without ongoing data, it is difficult to compare the

---

[49] Mike Leiter Director NCTC, hearing before the Senate HSGAC "Confronting the Terrorist Threat to the Homeland," September 30, 2009.

[50] Eric Schmitt, "New Teams Connect Dots of Terror Plots," *New York Times*, January 29, 2010.

[51] The Department of Homeland Security's (DHS) "Countering Violent Extremism Working Group" has taken steps to encourage partnerships with faith-based groups as part of their community policing initiative. The working group recently published recommendations which included studying the processes and ideological components of radicalization further, however at the time of publication, it is unclear to what extent their recommendations will be implemented and whether they will sufficiently address counter-radicalization.
See "Countering Violent Extremism (CVE) Working Group, Homeland Security Advisory Council," *Department of Homeland Security,* Spring 2010,
http://www.dhs.gov/xlibrary/assets/hsac_cve_working_group_recommendations.pdf

[52] Ahmad, page 255.

[53] "Muslim Americans: Middle Class and Mostly Mainstream," *Pew Research Center,* 2007.

[54] Zahid Bukhari, "Demography, Identity, Space: Defining American Muslims," in *Muslims in the United States: Demography, Beliefs, and Institution*, edited by Philippa Strum and Danielle Tarantolo, Woodrow Wilson International Center for Scholars, June 18, 2003.

direction or mood of American Muslims over time. Likewise, previous anthropological research does not provide policymakers with a holistic portrait of Muslims in America because they typically focus on a particular demographic group.

Akbar Ahmad's recent research, *Journey into America*, broke this trend by visiting over 100 mosques in 75 cities in America; however additional work and cross-national data is needed, especially in relation to sociological and cultural norms of various Muslim communities. Finally, the practice of Islam in America and the rise of radicalization have been under-researched and underfunded in part because radicalization is perceived to be a politically taboo subject. For years, national Muslim groups vehemently objected to the discussion, denying the existence of radicalization. Muslim leaders who challenged this view by exposing the influence of Islamist ideology in America were ostracized for dividing the Muslim community.[55] Even recently, policymakers keen on improving relations with Muslim communities have been careful to tread around the issue.[56] For example, in the 2010 National Security Strategy, President Obama avoided the issue almost entirely by omitting any references to radical Islam.[57] Unfortunately, the issue cannot be discussed fully until it is directly confronted by both Muslim and policymaking communities.

> Policymakers along with the American public require information on how the problem of radicalization has evolved in the US and abroad.

RECOMMENDATION 1.1 Increase Research on Radicalization

Public and private foundations should fund research on all aspects of radicalization to enable policymakers to create a diversified counter-radicalization strategy. Funding should be prioritized towards projects that explore various Islamist ideologies that lead to radicalization and how those ideologies are disseminated. Policymakers along with the American public will also require information on how the problem of radicalization has evolved in the US and abroad.[58] In addition, research on the factors that lead people to join (and leave) terrorist organizations are essential for constructing deradicalization policies. Finally, current deradicalization strategies led by moderate Muslims should be catalogued and studied, and benchmarks should be created to assess the efficacy of these efforts to determine how best to replicate them elsewhere.

RECOMMENDATION 1.2 Increase Research on Muslim Public Opinion

To better understand Muslim attitudes, public opinion institutions should engage Muslim communities on a number of contemporary social and political issues. For example, research should be undertaken on challenges and threats that face Muslim communities, the reconciliation of Islamic and American values, Muslim identity issues in America, and barriers to integrating into mainstream American society. There should also be polling of individual Muslims to determine if they believe national Muslim organizations represent their interests. Data from these research studies could guide policymakers to create policies that take into consideration the underlying pressures and dynamics within American Muslim communities.

---

[55] Muhammad Hisham Kabbani, "The Muslim Experience in America is Unprecedented," *Middle East Quarterly*, June 2000 http://www.meforum.org/61/muhammad-hisham-kabbani-the-muslim-experience-in

[56] "Editorial: 'Islamic Terrorism' and the Obama Administration," *LA Times*, June 8, 2010, http://articles.latimes.com/2010/jun/08/opinion/la-ed-islam-20100608

[57] Hersh, Newsweek http://www.newsweek.com/2010/06/17/a-politically-correct-war.html

[58] "Rewriting the Narrative: An Integrated Strategy for *Counter-Radicalization*," *Washington Institute for Near East Policy*, Washington, DC, 2009 p. 17

RECOMMENDATION 1.3 Increase Research on Muslim Demographics
Public and private foundations should fund research that develops a deep understanding of social, cultural and political demographics of Muslim communities (including both immigrant and indigenous populations) at the grass-roots community level. This data will enable local, state and federal government officials to acquire a richer understanding of the dynamics of Muslim communities, and identify potential partners for community-led counter-radicalization projects. With the proper research, decision-makers will be able to engage confidently with diverse communities and provide them the necessary support to better adapt into American society.

2. Moving Beyond Grievance Based Relations to Building a Partnership Against Radicalization

As described in publicly available sources, the present US government strategy to build relations with Muslim communities is centered around outreach efforts that are grievance-based (focusing on civil liberties), and are usually held on an ad-hoc basis. According to a report by the US Senate Committee on Homeland Security and Governmental Affairs (HSGAC), "The FBI's outreach program is not specifically designed to prevent the violent Islamist ideology from inspiring homegrown attacks, nor should it be… Rather, [FBI Director Robert Mueller believes] the FBI program is designed to promote confidence in the government as a whole and, more specifically, the FBI."[59] Similar efforts are currently undertaken by the Civil Rights and Civil Liberties (CRCL) at the Department of Homeland Security which meets with religious and ethnic community leaders in approximately five major cities to address their concerns. Although policymakers have found these types of meetings to be beneficial to establishing relationships and promoting dialogue, they are self-initiated, and not part of a government-wide effort to address radicalization.[60] These efforts should be replicated by other agencies, coordinated across additional major cities, and held with grass-roots Muslim organizations and community leaders to address the challenges of radicalization.

While national Muslim organizations have vast resources, they do not represent large segments of the US Muslim population- particularly local mosques and culturally Muslim groups - and as such, focusing on those groups alone risks alienating large segments of the US Muslim population.[61] Therefore, outreach initiatives should be expanded to include actors from a diverse cross-section of the American Muslim population. Moreover, better relationships at the local level will enable policymakers at the federal, state and local agencies to develop a coordinated response to counter-radicalization in *collaboration* with Muslim communities.

> Government outreach initiatives should empower Muslims at the grass-roots level to become the country's first line defense against homegrown terrorism.

RECOMMENDATION 2.1: Various Forms of Government Outreach at the Community Level
Public policymakers and government officials at the federal, state and local level should host town-hall meetings, listening tours and other traditional outreach approaches to facilitate relationships with

---

[59] Violent Islamist Extremism, the Internet, and the Homegrown Terrorist Threat – US HSGAC- majority/minority staff report May 8, 2008, 15.
[60] *Ibid*, page 14.
[61] Daniel Pipes and Sharon Chadha, "CAIR: Islamists Fooling the Establishment," *The Middle East Quarterly*, Spring 2006, 13:2, pages 3-20.

communities at the local level. Outreach efforts should be improved so that policymakers can better identify and work with Muslims who reflect the diversity of Islam in America, and uphold pluralistic and socially responsible ideological principals. Effective liaisons should be developed between key community leaders such as religious and cultural center leaders, teachers, businessmen, academics, as well as prison and military chaplains. These leaders have a great amount of influence and social capital because they have earned the trust of their community members. As a result, they have the greatest potential to serve as intermediaries with the government.

RECOMMENDATION 2.2: Government Outreach Outside of the Scope of Terrorism
In the past, federal, state and local law enforcement agencies have approached the problem of homegrown terrorism "from the outside-in," by bringing undercover informants into mosques to apprehend terrorist suspects. Unfortunately this approach has engendered a culture of paranoia and distrust between Muslims and the government.[62] According to 2007 public opinion data from the Pew Research Center, "Government anti-terrorism efforts are seen as singling out Muslims - and most of those who express this view are bothered by the extra scrutiny."[63] Without trust, local Muslims are hesitant to reach out to organizations like the FBI, making community level interventions difficult.[64]

Federal, state and local government officials should undertake new outreach efforts to build relationships with Muslim communities in an environment of mutual trust and respect. In addition, law enforcement agencies, and government officials should engage Muslim communities on issues of mutual interest outside of the scope of terrorism and community grievances, such as bullying in school, protecting children against online predators, maintaining public safety and engendering public service. This will broaden the basis for establishing community level relationships with Muslim communities, and increase civic engagement.

RECOMMENDATION 2.3: Establish a two- way Dialogue to Develop a Community Based Response to Radicalism.
A new, cooperative approach should include a series of two-way dialogues, constructive debates, and brainstorming sessions between federal, state and local law enforcement agencies, analysts, academics and Muslim community leaders. The dialogue should help participants understand the ideology of radical Islamists and how they are able to recruit, indoctrinate, and incite their followers to commit acts of violence. Specifically the dialogue participants should focus on how to understand and halt the radicalization process, and how to address other emerging threats. In particular, Muslim dialogue participants should facilitate a community based response to reduce radical Islamist's recruitment, develop counter-narratives to radical rhetoric, and stage interventions for at-risk persons.

3. Defining a Set of Shared Values:

Public-private partnerships specifically created to counter-radicalization should be made with Muslims who reject the uncompromising nature of radical Islamist doctrine and abhor its potential for violence. This does not mean that other government outreach relationships should cease to exist; it simply means

---

[62] "California Case Highlights FBI's Use of Mosque Spies." *MSNBC.com, March 2, 2009,* http://www.msnbc.msn.com/id/29461484/
[63] "Muslim Americans: Middle Class and Mostly Mainstream," *Pew Research Center,* 2007, page 10.
[64] James Dao and Eric Lichtblau, "Case Adds to Outrage for Muslims in Northern Virginia." *New York Times.* February 27, 2007, http://www.nytimes.com/2005/02/27/national/nationalspecial3/27terror.html?_r=1&pagewanted=2

that these partnerships should be based on a set of shared values. These values should counter the three key principles of radical ideologues: religious intolerance, the centrality of *military jihad* to Islamic practices, and the imposition of Islamist law in the US legal system.[65] Thought leaders, academics, organizations and activists who commit to these shared values are best positioned to exert pressure from within Muslim communities to moderate radicalized individuals and at risk persons.

RECOMMENDATION 3.1: Muslim Partners Should Support Religious Freedom
For example, all partners should publicly express their commitment to the inalienable right of religious freedom for all people in the US. In particular, Muslim partners should prohibit religious coercion and the practice of denouncing people as non-believers and apostates. Moreover, partners should publicly express the right of Muslims and non-Muslims to practice their various denominations without fear of persecution, discrimination or social alienation.

> Shared values should include supporting religious freedom, non-violent conflict resolution, and the preservation of the US Constitution.

RECOMMENDATION 3.2: Muslim Partners Should Support Non-Violent Conflict Resolution and Condemn Suicide bombing
Muslim partners should uphold the value of non-violent conflict resolution and wholly condemn suicide attacks (including countries where conflicts currently exists like Israel, Iraq, Somalia, Yemen and Afghanistan) as well as denounce all other forms of terrorism. Specifically, they should reject the centrality of military *jihad* to Islamic practices. For example, potential partners should publicly declare that the US' countering violent extremist agenda and the wars in Iraq and Afghanistan, do *not* justify a global military *jihad* for Muslims. Instead, partners should demonstrate their support for the common goal of defeating terrorists who threaten peace and stability worldwide. Rather than encouraging young people to join military *jihad* in Iraq, Pakistan, Somalia, or Afghanistan, young people should be encouraged to lead community service projects in their communities. Community leaders should facilitate productive civic engagement, and research towards peaceful, practical solutions to contemporary crises.

RECOMMENDATION 3.3: Muslim Partners Should Support the US Constitution and Rule of Law
Counter-radicalization partners should also publicly commit to preserving and maintaining the US Constitution and its system of governance. Policymakers should be wary of groups that are unwilling to publicly support the separation of church and state and whose goal may be to subvert the US rule of law and change America into a nation governed by Islamist law. Ideal partners should demonstrate their commitment to forging an American Muslim identity that is compatible with a democratic, pluralistic, open society.

4. Community-led, Earlier Interventions

In October 2006 the FBI received a tip about two individuals who had been known to frequently watch terrorist videos online. US citizens Mohamed Alessa and Carlos Almonte had self-radicalized online, listening to videos and recordings of the American-born cleric Anwar al-Awlaki that promoted

---

[65] These values are not intended to supplant current criteria for Muslim community engagement that addresses specific issues such as civil liberties or other law enforcement matters. Instead, this is a baseline criterion for a more collaborative, mutually reinforcing, counter-radicalization partnership.

{ Radical ideologies are becoming *the* determinant in the global war on terror – more so than militants' operational capacities }

martyrdom and killing innocent civilians in the course of waging violent *jihad*.[66] Their computers had documents written by terrorist organizers, including Usama bin Laden and Ayman al-Zawahiri, and their phones contained similar downloaded recordings. Drawn by videos of militants in Somalia carrying AK47 assault rifles and rocket propelled grenade launchers, three-and-a-half years later the two men planned to travel to Somalia to join the Al-Shabab, a terrorist organization with ambitions to topple Somalia's transition government and install a Taliban-like Islamic emirate.[67] Just before boarding their planes on June 5, 2010, the FBI arrested Alessa and Almonte for conspiring to commit acts of murder and kidnapping. In the Almonte and Alessa case, federal investigators spent three-and-a-half years building their case. What if local community members, in partnership with federal, state and local government officials were to have intervened earlier to actively turn the two young men away from their radical ideologies? Earlier interventions should be pursued because they have the potential to save lives as well as taxpayer dollars. The challenge is knowing which stage of radicalization to intervene.

A report by the New York Police Department indicates that the process of radicalization is often triggered by a life-changing experience – *e.g.,* bankruptcy, an incident of racism, the passing of family member, a romantic rebuff – that leads to a self-exploration of religion.[68] Prior to this pursuit, most recruits have an inadequate understanding of Islam, which makes them vulnerable to misinterpretations of religious doctrine. The individual may begin with audio CDs, books and the internet to inform themselves and then later may move on to "guided religious seeking" by clerics from a radical movement.[69]

According to Venhaus, "Al-Qaeda's ubiquitous message of anti-Muslim oppression and global *jihad* appeals to the developmental needs of adolescents."[70] Youth are drawn to radical, puritanical ideologies that attribute the poor state of Muslim communities – *e.g.* drone attacks in Pakistan, or civil strife in Gaza or Chechnya – to the amorality of society and failure to practice true Islam. Over time, the individuals believe that violence, as sanctioned in radical Islamist texts, is the only way to correct the state of affairs. As a result, radical ideologies are becoming *the* determinant in the global war on terror – more so than militants' operational capacities.[71]

---

[66] Robert Worth, "Cleric in Yemen Admits Meeting Airliner Plot Suspect, Journalist Says," *New York Times*, January 31, 2010, http://www.nytimes.com/2010/02/01/world/middleeast/01yemen.html?ref=umar_farouk_abdulmutallab

[67] "Foreign Terrorist Organizations," *US State Department*, http://www.state.gov/s/ct/rls/other/des/123085.htm, Accessed June 15, 2010.

[68] Mitchell Silber and Arvin Bhatt, "Radicalization in the West: The Homegrown Threat," *New York City Police Department,* 2007.

[69] Quintan Wiktorowicz, "Joining the Cause: Al-Muhajiroun and Radical Islam," Paper presented at "The Roots of Islamic Radicalism" Conference, Yale University, May 8-9, 2004. http://insct.syr.edu/Projects/islam-ihl/research/Wiktorowicz.Joining%20the%20Cause.pdf

[70] John Venhaus, "Why Youth Join al-Qaeda," *United States Institute for Peace Special Report*, May 2010.

[71] Sebastian Gorka, "The Surge that Could Defeat Al-Qaeda," *Foreign Policy,* August 10, 2009, http://www.foreignpolicy.com/articles/2009/08/10/the_one_surge_that_could_defeat_al_qaeda

Before such at-risk individuals resort to violence, there is a critical opportunity to intervene. Saudi clerics found that when they waited too long it was harder to rehabilitate hardened militants in prison, than those who were in the initial stages of radicalization.[72] Intervening before an individual becomes a "*jihadi*" is critical because the initial stages are when the individual is most impressionable and influenced by radical theological arguments. Intervening after an individual has become a *jihadi* and has joined a militant group is additionally challenging because of the individual's increased barriers to exit the group. For example, for individuals who have spent extensive time in radical groups, their decision to leave the group will depend on their consideration of the cost of time and effort already invested in the group, fear about reprisals from the group, and lack of protection against former enemies.[73] Moreover, even if individuals no longer believe in the group's ideology or political goals, they find leaving the group akin to leaving a family, community or an identity.[74] In short, the decision to leave a radical group becomes more difficult the longer someone has been radicalized.

> In the early stages of radicalization, young Muslims require access to credible, mainstream Muslim narratives that counter radical ideologies and promote moderation, pluralism and social cohesion.

RECOMMENDATION 4.1: Moderate Muslim Scholars Should Counter Radical Narratives

In the early stages of radicalization, young Muslims require access to credible, mainstream Muslim narratives that counter radical ideologies and promote moderation, pluralism and social cohesion. Using the framework of traditional and modern adaptations of Islamic teachings, texts and pedagogies, previous research indicates that moderate Muslim scholars have the capacity to provide legitimate counseling, counter-radicalization programming, and the religious retraining necessary to substantially curtail the radicalization process. Their success is attributed to their ability to provide an authentic religious paradigm that is palatable to at-risk and radicalized Muslims.[75] In other words, moderate Muslim scholars tend to be successful in countering radicalism because they are familiar with the culture, language, and arguments that radical clerics use and can provide an accurate rebuttal to each argument, point-by-point.[76] Community and religious centers can also provide religious retraining for at-risk youth. As educational facilities, they can provide American Muslims with the "talking points" they need to accurately represent mainstream Islam within their communities.

---

[72] Anne Speckhard, "Prison and Community Based Disengagement and De-Radicalization Programs for Extremists Involved in Militant *Jihadi* Terrorism Ideologies and Activities," Topical Strategic Multi-layer Assessment (SMA) Multi-Agency and Air Force Research Laboratory Multi-Disciplinary White Papers in Support of Counter-Terrorism and Counter –WMD, January 2010, page 348.

[73] Darcy M.E. Noricks, "Disengagement and Deradicalization: Process and Programs," in *Social Science for Counter Terrorism: Putting the Pieces Together,* edited by Paul Davis and Kim Cragin, RAND Corporation, 2009, page 302.

[74] *Ibid*, page 302.

[75] Hedieh Mirahmadi, Mehreen Farooq and Waleed Ziad, "Traditional Muslim Networks: Pakistan's Untapped Resource in the Fight Against Terrorism," WORDE, May 2010, page 22.

[76] Qamar ul-Huda "Peacemaking Efforts by Religious Actors," Topical Strategic Multi-layer Assessment (SMA) Multi-Agency and Air Force Research Laboratory Multi-Disciplinary White Papers in Support of Counter-Terrorism and Counter –WMD, January 2010, page 334-335.

RECOMMENDATION 4.2: Community Centers Should Provide Civic Education and Community Engagement Opportunities

Young Muslims require an outlet for their social and political frustration.[77] Community centers, run by Muslims and non-Muslims, should fill the dangerous vacuum of social and political apathy by providing young Muslims with civic engagement training to take ownership of their communities and to become responsible, peacefully engaged citizens in their local and international communities. For example, in the case of the "Virginia Five," the group of young men convicted of a terrorism plot in June 2010, one of the young men recorded a video before leaving for Pakistan in which he stated that young Muslims have a responsibility to do something in response to all the conflicts around the world.[78] Young men like him need access to mentors and community leaders who preach socially responsible definitions for what it means to be a "good Muslim." Unfortunately, even well-educated young Americans who are frustrated with the current state of affairs of Muslim communities are unaware of the Islamic values of conflict resolution and non-violence, as well as the countless avenues of peaceful involvement in shaping US foreign policy, or working through international development organizations abroad.

> Community centers can help immigrants socially adapt and can provide access to mentors and community leaders who preach socially responsible definitions for what it means to be a "good Muslim."

RECOMMENDATION 4.3: Public and Private Foundations Should Support Community Centers' Counter-Radicalization Efforts

The government should encourage private foundations and the business sector to provide support for community centers founded by moderate Muslims (or centers that agree to cater to the Muslim community), that will commit to the counter-radicalization process.[79] This recommendation is in line with the Homeland Security Council 2007 suggestion to prevent radicalization by "supporting community and grassroots efforts to promote the values of citizenship, democracy, integration, religious tolerance, and the protection of civil rights."[80]

Research by Schanzer *et al*, confirms that youth centers are an integral component to building strong communities that can counter-radicalization and provide guidance and positive experiences for youth.[81] Such centers can provide young Muslims alternative programs to focus their energy (*e.g.*, through sports, creative arts, political participation,

> For at-risk and formerly radicalized youth who have felt they have nowhere else to go, community centers can foster a sense of belonging and help build a positive self-identity that complements shared American and Islamic values.

---

[77] *Ibid.*

[78] Steven Stanek, "Missing Young Muslim Americans Held in Pakistan," *The National*, December 11, 2009. http://www.thenational.ae/apps/pbcs.dll/article?AID=/20091211/FOREIGN/712109870/0/HOUSE_HOME

[79] Private and public foundations should choose partners that support shared values and who *reject* three key principles of radical ideologues: religious intolerance, the centrality of military *jihad* to Islamic practices, as well as the wholesale replacement of the US constitution with extreme Islamist law.

[80] "National Strategy for Homeland Security," Homeland *Security Council*, October 2007, Page 22.

[81] David Schanzer, Charles Kurzman and Ebrahim Moosa, "Anti-Terror Lessons of Muslim-Americans," *Triangle Center on Terrorism and Homeland Security*, January 2010, http://www.sanford.duke.edu/news/Schanzer_Kurzman_Moosa_Anti-Terror_Lessons.pdf

or community volunteering) and a place to belong where they can address issues of social alienation. For at-risk and formerly radicalized youth who have felt they have nowhere else to go, community centers can foster a sense of belonging.[82] This is particularly important for those individuals who have left a radical group (after years of involvement), and who require a place where they can gain social acceptance, and integrate themselves into a positive social network. At the same time, such centers will also help American Muslims build a positive self-identity that complements shared American and Islamic values.[83]

5. Empowering Moderate Muslims to Counter Radical Ideology

Many young Muslims do not realize that radical clerics have not received substantial religious education and are largely unversed in the 1,400 years of debates and scholastic work on interpreting Islamic scriptures. Nonetheless charismatic radical clerics often appear as learned scholars to at-risk youth because of their ability to quickly cite verses from the Quran, and use sayings and traditions of the Prophet Muhammad to justify their positions.[84] Moderate Muslim scholars who are capable of countering radical ideology should be empowered to provide religious re-education for radicalized youth.

Throughout the world, moderate Muslim leaders have led the fight in countering radicalism by mobilizing millions in country-wide campaigns and issuing religious proclamations that categorically condemn suicide attacks and terrorism. The most prominent of the proclamations which received international attention was the 600-page fatwa condemning terrorism issued by Dr. Tahir ul Qadri, one of the world's leading moderate Muslim scholars. This fatwa, endorsed by the mainstream Muslim religious leadership across Pakistan, has been described as "arguably the most comprehensive theological refutation of Islamist terrorism to date."[85] An example within the US is the *fatwa* issued by the well-known scholar, Shaykh Hisham Kabbani, "Principles of Leadership in War and Peace" which categorically rejected the validity of military *jihad* today. The *fatwa* was translated into Arabic and was distributed by the US military to combat insurgency in Iraq.

> Local leaders are the best placed to intervene because they are aware of the dynamics within their community and can identify when someone displays disturbing behavior or radical opinions

Many Muslim leaders are active in promoting Islam as a religion of social cohesion and harmony – in direct contrast to their Islamist counterparts who preach victimization, hatred, and intolerance. While radical groups tend to support militant *jihad* and challenge existing political establishments by advocating for *Sharia*-based Islamic states, moderate Muslim leaders recognize that there is no validity to military *jihad* today and they vocally support working within existing state structures. As such, they are often very good resources for state officials interested in working with Muslim groups.

---

[82] Darcy M.E. Noricks, "Disengagement and Deradicalization: Process and Programs," in *Social Science for Counter Terrorism: Putting the Pieces Together,* edited by Paul Davis and Kim Cragin, RAND Corporation, 2009, page 302.
[83] Pakistani Political Action Committee (PAKPAC) Newsletter, December 22, 2009.
[84] Denis Mac Eoin, "Anwar al-Awlaki: 'I Pray that Allah Destroys America,'" *Middle East Quarterly*, Spring 2010, http://www.meforum.org/2649/anwar-al-awlaki-pray-allah-destroys-america
[85] "Cleric Issues Anti-Terror Fatwa," *AlJazeera.net*, March 2, 2010, http://english.aljazeera.net/news/europe/2010/03/2010321321826236.html

In Muslim-majority countries, moderate Muslims have a strong network of established institutions, and are able to deliver these counter-radicalization messages through their schools, mosques and social-welfare organizations. The challenge in America is that moderates are not as well-institutionalized. Unfortunately, many of these moderate individuals and groups lack the financial and political resources to mount a serious defense against their powerful, well-funded, and sophisticated adversary. As discussed above, Islamist institutions have greater funding sources from Gulf States, and as a result have attracted greater national attention from the media and policymakers.

RECOMMENDATION 5.1: Strengthen the Capacity of Moderate Muslim Networks to Counter Radicalization within Their Communities
In order to strengthen mainstream Muslim networks to become the "front line" defense against radicalization, the US Government can facilitate private partnerships that would strengthen the capacity of moderate Muslim networks. According to research by Schanzer *et al*, the stronger these organizations are, "in terms of social networks, educational programs, and provision of social services, the more likely they are to identify individuals who are prone to radicalization and intervene appropriately."[86]

Local leaders are the best placed to intervene when someone in their community is radicalized because they are aware of the dynamics within their community, have established relationships with their constituents, and can identify when someone displays disturbing behavior or radical opinions.[87] In the UK, policymakers found that when moderate community leaders were empowered, they were "better equipped to effectively reject the ideology of violent extremism, to isolate apologists of terrorism and to provide support to vulnerable institutions and individuals."[88] Similarly, within the US there should be programs funded by the Office of Faith-Based Initiatives, United States Institute for Peace (USIP), the National Endowment for Democracy (NED), and US universities to develop moderate Muslims' leadership and institutional capacity-building skills. They should also provide media training and communication development skills, as well as organizational marketing techniques. This will improve mainstream Muslims' ability to raise awareness of the counter-arguments to radical Islamism.

RECOMMENDATION 5.2: Public Officials Should Commend Muslim's Efforts to Counter Radicalization

> The work of moderate Muslim networks needs to be magnified in the public eye, and their voices need to be amplified to discredit radicals.

Public policymakers, government and law enforcement officials at the federal, state and local level should exert greater efforts to recognize and support the ongoing work of grassroots Muslim leaders and organizations to counter-radicalization. According to Ahmad, thousands of moderate Muslims have "sacrificed their lives to the violence perpetuated by the extremists... An internet search will yield tens of thousands of statements and press releases

---

[86] David Schanzer, Charles Kurzman and Ebrahim Moosa, "Anti-Terror Lessons of Muslim-Americans," *Triangle Center on Terrorism and Homeland Security*, January 2010, http://www.sanford.duke.edu/news/Schanzer_Kurzman_Moosa_Anti-Terror_Lessons.pdf

[87] Qamar ul-Huda "Peacemaking Efforts by Religious Actors," Topical Strategic Multi-layer Assessment (SMA) Multi-Agency and Air Force Research Laboratory Multi-Disciplinary White Papers in Support of Counter-Terrorism and Counter –WMD, January 2010, page 334-335.

[88] "The Prevent Strategy: A Guide for Local Partners in England; Stopping People Becoming or Supporting Terrorists and Violent Extremists," *HM Government*, June 20, 2008, page 31.

emphatically condemning terrorism. Yet few of them appear in the Western media, and any that do are drowned in the flood of Islamophobic sentiment."[89] The work of moderate Muslim networks needs to be magnified in the public eye, and their voices need to be amplified to discredit radicals. For example, federal, state and local policymakers can promote the work of moderate Muslims on their public websites, publications, and highlight their work in key speeches.

Policymakers and federal, state and local government officials can also work with leaders of the Muslim community to host dinners of outstanding recognition or award ceremonies of local mosque communities who have positively contributed to counter-radicalization efforts. Highlighting the powerful voice of Muslim leaders and their efforts will illustrate a positive example for Muslim youth to emulate. Finally, the public profile should be raised of groups that promote shared American values such as the freedom of religious expression, human liberty and dignity, as well as the freedom to assemble and express oneself. These groups should receive additional funding from public or semi-public foundations, as well as partnership opportunities with the US government. This form of recognition can engender cooperation and trust between the government and Muslim groups.

6. Creating Deradicalization Resources

In the 2007 Homeland Security report, the council urged "all levels of our government [to] strengthen institutions and human resources in a way that increases our ability to prevent violent Islamic extremism within our borders, identify when it is occurring, and spot new trends and developments in the radicalization process."[90] Policymakers need a systematic way of identifying religious and "culturally" Muslim networks (groups who identify with being Muslim but whose mission and organizational focus is not religious) that they can work with. US policymakers and law enforcement officials need a comprehensive toolkit that identifies the resources available to understand and address the pathways to radicalization.

> Without properly identifying these mainstream resources in the US, the government risks empowering the wrong groups, alienating local populations and turning potential allies into opponents.

RECOMMENDATION 6.1: Create a Resource for Policymakers that Identifies Muslim Partners
The toolkit should include a directory of Muslim leaders across the US who are committed to the shared values outline above and whose cultural, civic, and religious institutions can serve as government resources. The list should explore the scope of these organizations and their capacity to become involved with preventing violent extremism in their local communities. The list will help transition the government from working predominantly with the large national Muslim organizations, to reaching a larger cross-section of American Muslim communities. In addition, this list will facilitate community level dialogues and engender greater trust and cooperation between American Muslim citizens and the US government.

Without properly identifying these mainstream resources in the US, the government risks empowering the wrong groups, alienating local populations and turning potential allies into opponents. This directory should be compiled with the assistance of Muslims who have consistently denounced terrorism, religious radicalism, armed *jihad* in *any* country, and who promote religious diversity and freedom.

---

[89] Akbar Ahmad, page 438.
[90] "National Strategy for Homeland Security," Homeland *Security Council*, October 2007, page 23.

These individuals should have a demonstrated desire to work with the state, and observe shared principals of democracy, civic engagement, and pluralism. This list should be made public and available for use by city and state government officials as well as civil society actors who are interested in public/private community level partnerships to counter radicalism.

RECOMMENDATION 6.2: Establish an Educational Forum on Islam
In addition to a directory, the government should create an educational forum where local leaders, religious scholars, academics and analysts can brief local and national policymakers about the difference between Islamic ideologies and the pathways to radicalization in America. These forums should be a two-way dialogue where the participants can discuss how to recognize red flags and how to pair local communities with the resources they need to address the threats. Finally, the forums should enable policymakers to identify the best community-led solutions so they can be replicated across the country. A good place to start could be hosting these discussions at law enforcement "fusion centers" that are already tasked with the counterterrorism portfolio.

7. A Public Awareness Campaign

Given the increased attention of homegrown terrorism in the media, and the misunderstandings between Muslims and non-Muslims in America, it is important to engage in a national dialogue to counter the misperception that all Muslims are radical. The recent uproar about the "Ground Zero Mosque" illustrates that the American public is increasingly uncomfortable with the role of Islam and Muslims in American society. Being honest about the threat from radical ideology will help the average American understand the difference between mainstream Islam and its perversion.

RECOMMENDATION 7.1: Initiate a National Dialogue to Define the Challenges of Radicalization in America
Policymakers in the White House, Capitol Hill, and federal agencies should announce a national dialogue to discuss the variations of Islamic ideologies, elucidating the differences between radical and mainstream religious tenets. The national dialogue should clearly expose the threat of radical ideologies that breed intolerance and hatred, which endangers the life of peaceful citizens both Muslim and non-Muslim alike. The campaign should create an awareness of the tenets that separate this politically motivated doctrine from the spiritual, theology of Islam as practiced by the majority of Muslims around the world.

RECOMMENDATION 7.2: Create Public Forums and Conferences to Facilitate the National Dialogue

> By including all major Muslim stakeholders who agree upon the aforementioned shared values, there will be a broad-based community buy-in and a diverse set of ideas and strategies presented.

Public policymakers and federal officials should organize town hall meetings, conferences and seminars that bring the public together with experts and Islamic scholars from a broad spectrum of viewpoints –including Sufis, Shi'as, apolitical Salafis, and culturally Muslim groups - to address the threat of domestic radicalization. By including all major Muslim stakeholders who agree upon the aforementioned shared values, there will be a broad-based community buy-in and a diverse set of ideas and strategies presented .The forum will demonstrate to the American people that important contributions are being made by the American Muslim community to solve the problem. In the process, it will also reveal the doctrinal differences between mainstream Muslims and the radicals. These forums can be televised on major news outlets to ensure broad publicity. The information generated should be disseminated through public channels including the internet, schools, college campuses, online forums and prisons.

RECOMMENDATION 7.3: Provide Public Forums Specifically for Muslims to Address Internal Community Challenges

Public and private foundations should also provide resources for Muslims to convene and discuss organic deradicalization efforts within their communities. In particular these conferences should highlight ways in which Muslim communities can develop a bottom-up strategy to countering radicalization. Hearings should also be hosted on the Hill to describe "best practices" from cities across America.

RECOMMENDATION 7.4: Muslim Groups Should Issue National, Public Statements against Radicalism

Muslim groups in America should also develop public awareness campaigns to denounce radicalization. They should issue statements separately, or in conjunction with one another, that reject the three key principles of radical ideologues: religious intolerance, the centrality of *military jihad* to Islamic practices, and the imposition of Islamist law in the US legal system. Media and public officials should reference such statements to increase their dissemination.

As part of a broader effort to discredit radical interpretations of Islam, community-led initiatives should include the distribution of pamphlets, booklets and other material that emphasize Islamic values of allegiance to state authority, religious tolerance, pluralism, gender equality, as well as the importance of social cohesion, and overall social welfare.

8. Countering Narratives Online

The internet is an increasingly significant vehicle for radicalizing Muslims in America. According to the HSGAC, organizations like Al-Qaeda are increasing their production of English propaganda targeted at US and English speaking audiences.[91] For example, in June 2010, Al-Qaeda promoted the publication of their first English online magazine, "Inspire."[92] These organizations have a sophisticated operation which enables them to use multimedia to spread radical ideologies that justify terrorism and attract recruits at

> In conjunction with creating positive online spaces, local community centers and mosques should hold special programs to discuss the dangers of the online radicalization with young Muslims.

an unprecedented rate. Their success relies on an efficient business model. Content – a fiery sermon by a charismatic figure, or a video of a martyr and militant attacks – is first created by regional production centers and is then funneled through a clearinghouse to ensure authenticity before the content is distributed and posted on pre-approved websites. The websites are used to address, defend and legitimize followers' concerns, while acting as a vehicle to communicate their core message. Individuals can log in online and access virtual extremist schools where they can download books on the supposed theological justifications for violent Islamist ideology. They also use chat rooms and bulletin boards as networking resources, to connect with like-minded individuals. In addition, some sites feature

---

[91] "Violent Islamist Extremism, the Internet, and the Homegrown Terrorist Threat– US HSGAC- majority/minority staff Report" May 8, 2008, page 8.
[92] Catherine Herridge, "American Cleric Tied to Times Square and Christmas Day Bombing Attempts Gets New Website," *FoxNews.com*, June 30, 2010, http://www.foxnews.com/politics/2010/06/30/american-cleric-tied-times-square-christmas-day-bombing-attempts-gets-new/

videogames and other flashy, hi-tech, and interactive media that appeals to younger demographics. Unfortunately there are not enough online resources that counter the technologically advanced and popularly presented format of this material.

Some policy analysts believe that counterterrorism funds should not be diverted towards monitoring and blocking radical online websites because they believe that the processes of radicalization and recruitment are anchored in the real world.[93] Unfortunately, according to Lawrence Sanchez, the Assistant Commissioner of the New York Police Department's Intelligence Division, online space does play a significant role in the radicalization process – both for informing opinions, and for providing a resource portal for *jihadists*.[94]

RECOMMENDATION 8.1: Create Counter-Radicalization Websites

In addition to the efforts that are already being undertaken to reduce the number of radical websites, there is an opportunity to further reduce their impact by creating websites that educate Muslims on mainstream Islam and discredit radical arguments. Previous researchers have suggested that civil society should be funded to create online projects aimed at countering extremist messages.[95] Expanding on this idea, local Muslim leaders, imams and scholars should lead this effort and create online spaces to challenge radical theology and to make themselves available for people who need counseling. These websites should be controlled by local community leaders who have gained the respect and legitimacy from their community or by internationally renowned scholars who have the charisma and intellectual fortitude to take on the extremist dogma.

RECOMMENDATION 8.2: Create Radical Propaganda Awareness Programs

In particular, the new websites should emphasize that extremist propaganda is a perversion of Islam and does not represent the faith. Young Muslims should be encouraged to participate in positive online spaces, and to openly discuss their concerns and questions with their community leaders.

---

[93] "Countering Online Radicalization, A Strategy for Action," *International Center for the Study of Radicalization and Political Violence*.

[94] "Violent Islamist Extremism, the Internet, and the Homegrown Terrorist Threat– US HSGAC- majority/minority staff Report" May 8, 2008, page 12.

[95] Stevens, Tim and Dr. Peter R. Neumann. *Countering Online Radicalisation*. Kings College Press, London; United Kingdom, 2009, Page 49.

CHALLENGES

The strategy recommendations presented in this paper represent a holistic, long-term approach to a grave national security threat. Many of the recommendations are innovative approaches to the problem but are not without controversy and political sensitivity. Establishing relations with community leaders, identifying credible partners, and building up the institutional capacity of moderate Muslim networks will take considerable time and political will. There are other challenges as well.

A new national counter-radicalization strategy will require a paradigm shift in the way the US government responds to radicalization. Given the separation of religious institutions from public affairs, the US government has a strong legal and ethical trepidation about delving into matters deemed to be religious in nature. The role of ideology and theology in radicalization has been left in the hands of Muslims, whom policymakers believe are best equipped to deal with the problem, but who to date have been slow to address it. This presents a critical opportunity for the government to intervene. There needs to be political capital behind tackling the tough questions publicly and honestly. If the Administration were to announce a national conversation about radicalization, in partnership with the Muslim community and the private sector, it will generate the incentives necessary to confront the problem. Very few Muslim leaders would want to be excluded from such a high profile endeavor; and as the UK model illustrates, most will sign on to participate.

Another challenge is that, while moderate Muslims can lead the fight against radicalization, they tend to be underfunded and lack the necessary institutional capacity to effectively compete with Islamists. Previous research confirms that many moderate Muslim groups require leadership and communications training to maximize the impact of their message of peace and social cohesion.[96] Public-private partnerships against radicalization will have to strengthen their core capabilities in order to succeed.

Another challenge is the fear, or hesitation from Muslim communities to actively speak out against radicalization. Many Muslims are afraid to challenge radical Islamists out of fear of personal safety or being labeled as anti-Islamic or ignorant of Islamic tenets.[97] Others fear they will become ostracized by the community for airing Islam's 'dirty laundry' in the public. This can be resolved if the government were to lead the endeavor and establish a call for partnerships. The problem however is compounded by the perception that the small percentages of American Muslims who have faced physical violence from speaking out, have received little support from the justice system to prosecute their offenders.[98] Therefore, law enforcement agencies will have to ensure proper enforcement of hate crime legislation, (including crimes committed by Muslims against Muslims). At the same time, moderate Muslim organizations need to establish a consensus that it is essential to speak out against radicalization in order to preserve the true message of Islam.

Finally, it is likely that this new counter-radicalization strategy will receive a large push back from radical Islamists. In the UK, Islamists challenged the government's PREVENT strategy by claiming it was an attack on Islam. In their attempt to subvert the new strategy, they perpetuated the belief that the program would cultivate greater Islamophobia and hatred towards Muslims. Paradoxically, at the same

---

[96] Akbar Ahmad, page 233.
[97] "Torture for beer drinkers" By Mona Eltahawy, *Washington Post*, Tuesday, October 27, 2009.
[98] Akbar Ahmad, Page 235.

time they worked diligently to portray their organizations as moderate institutions that were credible partners for the government.[99]

Here in the US, prior to September 11, 2001, many national Muslim organizations openly criticized the US government for supporting the Arab-Israeli peace process, occasionally funded terrorist groups like Hamas, and actively worked against a variety of state interests. While their rhetoric may at times remain inflammatory and counterproductive, they still seek a relationship with the US government. Similar to the UK, the US should expect Islamist organizations in the US to vehemently object to the new strategy while at the same time seek to be a part of it. Therefore it is important to carefully scrutinize each organization the government wishes to partner with, examining their domestic and international funding sources and ties to radical groups. The government will have to examine the principles that American Muslim organizations and community leaders espouse, with particular attention to whether there was a genuine shift after 9-11. An ideal Muslim partner is one who supports the aforementioned shared values and who can consistently demonstrate a rejection of the three key principles of radical ideologues.

---

[99] Maajid Nawaz and Ed Husain, "Preventing Terrorism: Where Next for Britain?" *Quilliam Strategic Briefing Paper*, June 14, 2010.

CONCLUSION

The growing threat of homegrown terrorism in the US demands a reevaluation of our current approach to countering radicalization. While there are a number of routes to radicalization, an undeniable driving force is the problem of radical ideologies. In most of the recent cases of terrorism attempts in the US, radical interpretations of Islam were the underlying ideology that legitimized, justified and encouraged acts of terrorism. Policymakers will have to look beyond the traditional law enforcement approaches in which authorities intervene just before or after an act of terror and instead concentrate domestic resources to support community-led initiatives by moderate Muslims that deter individuals from radicalizing in the first place. This approach will save lives and taxpayer dollars.

Law enforcement agencies will also have to move beyond grievance-based forums of engagement to creating partnerships with Muslims who will lead the struggle against domestic radicalization. This approach also requires innovative research to better understand the threat so that the country can better prepare for the solution.

The importance of moderate, mainstream Muslims cannot be overemphasized. Both the Muslim community and the various government agencies involved need a mutually reinforcing platform from which to tackle the problem of radicalization. New partnerships must be guided by a commitment to the American ideals of religious liberty, human dignity, and preservation of the US constitution as the guiding principles of our government. Partners will need to publicly express their support for the initiative and demonstrate concrete actions to advance the program. In response, the American public will realize there are many members of the Muslim community just as concerned and committed to the fight against terrorism as non-Muslims. It is hoped that such an endeavor may finally heal the wounds of 9-11 and subsequent acts of terror, which have divided the American people on religious fault lines.

www.ingramcontent.com/pod-product-compliance
Lightning Source LLC
Chambersburg PA
CBHW051428070526
44584CB00023B/3631